T0195914

Also by Michael Baez

*How to Pick Your Bride and How to Keep Her for Life*
*How to Pick Your Bride and How to Keep*
*Her for Life: Hard Moments Journal*

# Her Heart

*Letter to Christian Men:*
*Understanding Your Bride's Heart*

## MICHAEL BAEZ

WESTBOW
PRESS®
A DIVISION OF THOMAS NELSON
& ZONDERVAN

Copyright © 2024 Michael Baez.

All rights reserved. No part of this book may be used or reproduced by any means, graphic, electronic, or mechanical, including photocopying, recording, taping or by any information storage retrieval system without the written permission of the author except in the case of brief quotations embodied in critical articles and reviews.

This book is a work of non-fiction. Unless otherwise noted, the author and the publisher make no explicit guarantees as to the accuracy of the information contained in this book and in some cases, names of people and places have been altered to protect their privacy.

WestBow Press books may be ordered through booksellers or by contacting:

WestBow Press
A Division of Thomas Nelson & Zondervan
1663 Liberty Drive
Bloomington, IN 47403
www.westbowpress.com
844-714-3454

Because of the dynamic nature of the Internet, any web addresses or links contained in this book may have changed since publication and may no longer be valid. The views expressed in this work are solely those of the author and do not necessarily reflect the views of the publisher, and the publisher hereby disclaims any responsibility for them.

Any people depicted in stock imagery provided by Getty Images are models, and such images are being used for illustrative purposes only. Certain stock imagery © Getty Images.

ISBN: 979-8-3850-1669-3 (sc)
ISBN: 979-8-3850-1670-9 (hc)
ISBN: 979-8-3850-1671-6 (e)

Library of Congress Control Number: 2024900778

Print information available on the last page.

WestBow Press rev. date: 2/9/2024

Scripture quotations marked NKJV are taken from the New King James Version. Copyright © 1982 by Thomas Nelson, Inc. Used by permission. All rights reserved.

Scripture quotations marked TLB are taken from The Living Bible copyright © 1971. Used by permission of Tyndale House Publishers, Inc., Carol Stream, Illinois 60188. All rights reserved.

Scripture quotations marked The Voice are taken from The Voice Bible Copyright © 2012 Thomas Nelson, Inc. The Voice™ translation © 2012 Ecclesia Bible Society All rights reserved.

Scripture quotations marked NIV are taken from the Holy Bible, New International Version®, NIV®. Copyright © 1973, 1978, 1984 by Biblica, Inc.™ Used by permission of Zondervan. All rights reserved worldwide.

Scripture quotations marked ESV are from the ESV Bible® (The Holy Bible, English Standard Version®), copyright © 2001 by Crossway Bibles, a publishing ministry of Good News Publishers. Used by permission. All rights reserved.

Scripture quotations marked KJV are taken from the Holy Bible, King James Version.

Scripture quotations taken from the New American Standard Bible®, Copyright © 1960, 1962, 1963, 1968, 1971, 1972, 1973, 1975, 1977, 1995 by The Lockman Foundation. Used by permission. (www.Lockman.org)

Scripture quotations in this publications are from The Message. Copyright © by Eugene H. Peterson 1993, 1994, 1995, 1996, 2000, 2001, 2002. Used by permission of NavPress Publishing Group.

Scripture quotations taken from the Revised Standard Version of the Bible, copyright ©1952 [2nd edition, 1971] by the Division of Christian Education of the National Council of the Churches of Christ in the United States of America. Used by permission. All rights reserved.

Scripture quotations taken from the Revised Standard Version of the Bible: Catholic Edition, copyright © 1965, 1966 the Division of Christian Education of the National Council of the Churches of Christ in the United States of America. Used by permission. All rights reserved.

Scripture quotations taken from the Inductive Study Bible NASB Copyright 1960, 1962, 1963, 1968, 1971, 1972, 1973, 1975, 1977 by The Lockman Foundation A Corporation Not for Profit La Habra, CA All Rights reserved. International copyright secured.

Scripture quotations taken from the International Inductive Study Bible Copyright 1992, 1993 Published by Harvest House Publishers 1075 Arrowsmith Eugene, Oregon 97402

*This book is dedicated to my Father, the Living God,
God Almighty, His perfect living example;
to my brother, Jesus, King of Kings, and to the Holy Spirit.*

*Special thanks to the Word, who gave me these words,
and to Christ's Helper who transmitted and
made these words a part of me.*

# Contents

# Preface

I have learned that God loves you very much and follows you wherever you go. So whatever activity we engage in, whether positive or negative, innocent or sinful, our Heavenly Father, Jesus, or the Holy Spirit is there. When you are loving your bride, God is there, and when you are fighting your bride, God is there. I have a positive memory as a Catholic attending grammar school a long time ago when I read Genesis and said to God in prayer, "Lord, I found the source of all the problems in the world. You changed us."

At that time, Genesis 3:7 did strike me as the source of all our earthly problems. I often watched war movies and news with my dad in the evenings, and I knew from the Bible that the Fall of Adam was the reason for so much of the death I saw. Scripture seemed to be telling me that before Adam and Eve ate the forbidden fruit, everything was good, and God was happy. It was not until they ate the wrong fruit that all the bad things we have to live with on earth became a reality. I thought about how I used to sweat on hot days and freeze on winter days and how the temperature before the Fall of Adam was always perfect. I wondered whether I would like that. I did not understand much about God then. Still, I knew that in a God-created perfect world, you could be perfectly comfortable wearing a light windbreaker jacket in a blizzard or a down coat walking in the Sahara on a scorching day. Let me know when you understand that!

Believing in the power of God and that God answered prayer, I simply asked God to forgive us and make us all like Adam and Eve before the Fall. As a fourth-grader who didn't understand the sin involved, I asked God, "If our bodies were good before, and there was no problem, why don't You do what You did before and make us have the bodies and non-sinful nature Adam had before his fall? Especially since You felt that was good. Problem solved!" No response from God to that question, and I continued my life.

More than fifty-five years later, and the reason my memory above is positive, I learned that God does answer all prayers and questions. Yes, Adam and Eve's physical bodies and hearts were perfect when God first created them, but I learned that we had a sinful nature since their fall. The Holy Spirit told me that thanks to our Father's work, the eye-opened fallen bodies and hearts of Adam and Eve were perfect for their new life outside the garden and God's purpose for us today.

The statement I made in prayer to God was not full of extraordinary knowledge or wisdom. It may have been my ability to observe the obvious, or perhaps it is just my internal mother provided natural ability to ask or take on a unique point of view. In truth, for a long time I was as clueless as everyone else on the heart of women until the Holy Spirit filled me with knowledge after my marriage. In one moment, it was an understanding greater than my brain could handle, and I had to type it all down. My first book was on how to give agape love. Although this book also touches on agape love, its purpose is to give male readers the reason for agape love.

The Holy Spirit used all my life experience to help explain agape love. My statement to God reveals a biblical understanding of the human heart before the Fall and after the Fall. Today it should be obvious which is better. It reveals a want and need for all of us to go back to the original state of heart we had before our individual fall. Successful use of the book you're reading may require going back to reread parts or the whole, and taking time to meditate on the words just as you meditate on the Bible. *Her Heart* goes deeper than my previous book, *How to Pick Your Bride and How to Keep Her for Life*, and focuses on the goal of understanding your bride. You chose her, but you don't know her. You may find yourself saying, "I don't understand her. Why is she the way she is? What are her secrets?" The truth is, even she may not know. But the answer is in *Her Heart*—the heart of your bride.

Your own original heart's desire is to save, to be the hero—to be like Jesus. Don't be afraid to ask for help from your pastor or a group of like-minded brothers in a church. Pursue your bride with precision acts of agape and with biblical understanding of her heart, the way Jesus is pursuing your heart. Persistent application is the key.

This book is for Christian men who are planning to marry and who already have some familiarity with the Bible. This book is also for married Christian men who are having trouble with their marriage. I believe there are successful marriages out there not necessarily in need of this book. But in my journeys through churches there are many couples I see in need of the Biblical approach my books teach. I am a witness to the married Christian men struggling in men's groups. Many asking me questions about their marriage my books answer. Marital knowledge though in the Bible seems to slip by readers heart process though they have gone to church and been married many years. I hope to awaken the men to what the Bible is really saying about marriage. Hoping to create a more peaceful, gentler marriage, enlightening readers how the wisdom and application of true Christ likeness, understanding the heart helps a man more easily handle the marital relationship. It is also for men who may know how to love their bride in the spirit of agape but are asking Christ for a reason to continue in what may seem at times like a lonely battle for love. Many teachers quoting the Bible quickly remind you that the heart is deceitful above all things, and desperately sick: *who can understand it?* The Bible does teach this negative view of the heart, but don't forget that the Bible also contains everything needed to understand *her heart* the way God originally made it and to treat the current fallen state of the heart. I hope it helps you to have a better marriage and to become a better husband, not just a man who has developed worldly argumentative skills to use against his bride.

If you develop a closer mindset to that of Christ, you can know how Christ feels about your bride and understand your bride's heart from Christ's point of view. When you are handling your married life from a more knowledgeable point of view, you will gain self-respect from the position of power Christ has placed you in.

The book is structured in two parts, with teachings in the first, and a second part that offers meditations for solidifying the Bible's teachings on how to stay married for life. An understanding of all the information God wants to provide us takes more than one lesson—it may take a lifetime. So I hope that you will read your Bible more to rediscover what God has been teaching over the many lifetimes of man's existence. And I hope you will learn what Christ knows: the secrets of *her heart.*

*Now, what the Holy Spirit revealed to me ...*

# A Letter to Christian Grooms

Dear Brothers in Christ,

Many people say the Bible is complicated and talks about many things. Could the Bible simply be about the Creator, our One True God who creates everything, needs nothing, but wants one thing? If you said, "He wants a kingdom," you are very close and that may be true—unlike other dead false gods who simply wanted pomp and circumstance, power, and authority over the human creation without having anything worthwhile to give to the people.

Most false gods are dead fallen angels who never understood what humans are built to want. They could not provide it because before they fell, they were angels who, as God's earlier creation, were not necessarily capable of understanding God's plan for them in full. This is revealed as you learn from the scriptures about the angel rebellion in heaven. They wanted power without the capability of knowing or understanding the love God had for them or knowing the love God wanted expressed in His kingdom. All the wonderful things in heaven were not enough for them.

The difference between our One True God of the Bible and other false gods is that, besides wanting a kingdom, the God of the Bible is searching for a relationship as close as a bride. For some Christians, this statement is easily understood. Others will have to go back to church to understand what a bride is. For those who have a basic understanding of what a bride is but still cannot understand the statement, I repeat: the God of the Bible wants a relationship with His creation as close as a bride: "Come, I will show you the bride, the wife of the Lamb" (Revelations 21:9 NIV). Christians believe the Lamb is the Messiah (Jesus), and the Bride is His church. Our Creator is searching for a relationship built on love for His creation that is as close as a father to his children and as close as a groom and his bride.

Our Creator, the God of the Bible, put this irremovable desire for God and godly love in each and every human creation born on earth. History reveals that nothing will satisfy this inner desire God put in us. While other false gods barely provide only material things, our Creator, God of the Bible, wants love, and for that love gives all grooms the Bride.

Write your bride's name here:

Could the whole Bible from the beginning to the end—God's creation of potential brides, making a place for them, and Christ's search for and redeeming His Bride—be about marriage? Could all the Bible's emphasis on sanctification be not only a requirement of our Creator God but also a help to the married couples who have dedicated their lives to each other?

If you are unsure whether the Bible is all about marriage, fast-forward to the end of the Bible. It leaves all readers who have completed the reading with the following unwritten question:

Will you marry Christ or not?

The Bible's whole purpose is to lead the reader to that question of marriage. The meaning of life is marriage—a mature but childlike equal/opposite marriage.

You can see the metaphor of the words *groom* and *bride*, but be sure to understand that God is not playing around. He takes His part of the relationship seriously and understands the problem we have with marriage. He has taken the time (many human lifetimes) to explain everything needed to make a successful lifelong marriage possible. The Bible reveals everything the

Creator had to do to make such a wedding possible. What He had to do sets the example of what we have to do, like creating a venue for the wedding to take place—the earth.

Some would say the Bride is the church. That is true if you understand the church as being the people in it, but if you think the wedding place is just a physical building God could have simply created a building in space. He offers the Bride much more than a building. Before the wedding, the Bible reveals God had to teach the fallen human beings about marriage, what it should entail, and what it should consist of. The Bible reveals instantly with the murder of Abel and onward that men and their families had no idea what marriage and love is. The Bible talks about marriage lessons to be learned, and the importance of leadership or serving in marriage. The Bible reveals that everyone should be married, yet it talks about whether you should be a groom, a bride, or single, and when grooms should be high priests and how. It talks about morality and marriage.

God had the most difficult time teaching His human grooms how to love. He taught what love is, the rules of love, and how love is an essential part of marriage. The Bible tells us how to be a groom, what qualities make up a perfect groom, and who the perfect groom is. It talks about what qualities make up a perfect bride and how to be a bride. It talks about whom to marry and the qualities you should look for in a spouse. It tells its readers who don't already know how to marry.

The Bible talks about what sin is and how it affects marriage, and how marriage requires righteousness, teaching what that is and how to be righteous. It talks about providing for the family, which eventually consists of brides and grooms.

Also included in the Bible are historical interactions between different grooms and brides, and the Creator and his prophets. The Bible details what to do and how to handle things when married couples grow into large families—towns, cities, and nations. It talks about married couples and war. It contains historical examples of marriage and past failures of marriages, and revealing arguments within married families, disputes, and battles outside the family. I did not include single people in this book because the Bible, in the end, encourages all to be married to Christ.

God's Book talks about material things, how the Bride and the Groom are more important than other things our hands or the Lord has created. The benefits of marriage are thoroughly talked about, as well as boldly hinting what marriages will succeed or fail. It reveals what you get when you marry Christ, the rewards of the wedding, and what happens when you don't marry Christ.

Again, the Bible's purpose is to prepare the reader for marriage. The marriage question: will you marry Christ or not?

The Bible reveals that the most important priority for the groom seeking and searching for love is knowing the Bride— knowing *her heart*!

# *Part One*

# Understanding
# Her Heart

# "I Don't Understand Her"

*Many a groom has* said of his bride, "I don't understand her." But to truly know your bride, you have to understand *her heart*.

It is best to start with you. The reason may offend, but it must be stated. Because of the Fall, men have become selfish creations, refusing to understand the other person's point of view. So to understand *her heart*, you first may have a need to understand your own heart. Could any of the following be you?

> *I know you.*
> *Hmm. Maybe just a part of you: your heart.*

Test me, and please read on. If you continue, you will know also what the Holy Spirit told me about your heart, *her heart*, my heart, and the heart of every human person in creation.

When you say you know someone's heart, it is taken to mean that you genuinely know them. Most people believe the brain, the mind, and the heart are what we use to make decisions in life—and they do contain our innermost thoughts and beliefs. In ancient Israel, when they spoke about the heart, they were talking about the brain. They felt the "heart" was the inner part of all people and contained the decision-making ability. Jesus in the New Testament said and proved that He could read the *heart* (Matthew 26:20–25). Although the word "mind" is also used in the Bible, I'll be using the word "heart" when I talk about discerning your bride.

The Bible repeatedly reveals that the heart is deceitful above all things and desperately wicked. Who can understand it (Jeremiah 17:9)? To understand the heart, it is essential to realize that the wicked parts of the heart are not the whole of it. Another part of the heart is the original, perfect, God-created, undivided heart. The details of the original heart are how I know you. You are not a fly-by-night chance; you are not a chemical reaction without a purpose. You were made for a reason. You were created, born, for *love*.

God loved His work as He was making you, and upon completion He said, "You are perfect." But on God's heart were five vital questions:

1. Will you see me?
2. Will you hear me?
3. Will you listen to me?
4. Will you want me?
5. Will you love me?

He then sent you to be born.

Don't rush through those five questions. Meditate on them for a moment and realize that God made you in His image. He put those vital questions in you. Like God, you have been mentally asking these vital questions all your life.

### *From Conception*

What did you want after you were conceived and inside your mother? Many of you were conceived inside your mother, and if there were no problems, sharp pains, or chemical burns, you were growing, at rest, possibly drifting in and out of sleep, in complete warmth, comfort, peace, and happiness, and you were fully fed. Not bothered by life. You may have discovered your body and touch. You may have liked the feeling and touched yourself all over. Putting parts of your body in your mouth. This was not sexual; at that time you were just learning you had a body. You did not even know what the parts were. And then you were born instinctively processing the vital questions God programmed into all of us. You were born knowing how to love, wanting to love, wanting to be wanted, loving to be loved, and constantly processing those previous vital questions. In the beginning, your program was intense, functioning, and vibrant. You were ready and willing to love, wanting to be wanted, but God put in one catch. God made you perfect; you were programmed to demand nothing less than an equally perfect heart from someone else who would return your love. You wanted another perfect heart to be with you always—*God's heart.*

Meditate on this for a moment. Try to think back, if you can, to your early self. How far back in your life do you have to go to find the real you, the you that God made? The way you once were before life hit you hard? Jesus died on the cross you so that you can return to that place.

Often people ask if I can recall the day when Jesus came to me and saved me. For the purpose of this chapter, I sadly ask you to recall the first of possibly many sins against your heart that changed you from your perfect God-created self, which existed when you were born.

## *Your Heart after You Are Born*

After you are born, you experience your first touch from someone outside the womb. I don't know how you reacted to being touched for the first time. You'd have to ask your doctor. If you were blessed, you were almost immediately placed in your mother's arms. She held you close. You felt and suckled your mother, and if your taste buds worked, you were happy.

Every moment in life, you use your senses. Life is in the senses, and touch may be the most powerful bonding sense God created in you. That is why God wrote such warnings of the flesh in the New Testament, as in Galatians 5:16 NIV: "So I say live by the Spirit, and you will not gratify the desires of the flesh." Warnings and teachings like these, which are now necessary and helpful, were not always so. From the beginning, God wanted you to have a sense of touch. The Old Testament reveals that God knew the sense of touch in a fallen state would break down the original heart program He created in Adam and Eve and in many people.

"Heart program?" many people may yell. "I am human, not a machine!" But the older I become, the more understanding of people I obtain, and the more mechanical in nature humans seem to become, made with now seemingly interchangeable modular parts, following what seems to be predictable actions, by our God who creates them with words. It is not hard to conclude that the heart and soul of a man is a unique system of words—a program— created by God, infused in such a way as to create life. It is not hard to see how the forbidden fruit contained a bunch of words to confuse and kill that life that God created.

For many people, the touch that God created would be so troublesome He had to offer His human creations a new option. The fact is, when you start seeking a bride and choose to touch a woman in the process before marriage, her heart's program starts to run wild. The questions of eternal love and more begin to form in her heart, possibly just when she sees you.

Let us reconstruct this question backwards. Many a groom has said of his bride, "I don't understand her." Clearly, any communication, good or bad, forces a person to think and immediately ask themselves the vital five vital questions to analyze the communication. You have meditated on those vital questions, have you not? If not, take a moment to reread them. The main purpose of those internal questions is not to force a flight or fight response but to analyze and find out whether you are loved. It is the main reason we all ask those five questions. When we answer, "Yes, we are being loved," we ask other questions, possibly with differences depending on whether we are men or women.

Secondary unique questions, often important to a woman's heart, have to do with security. I am not a women, and I am writing for other men. So try to imagine all the secondary questions running through a woman's heart when trying to analyze situations of touch, love, marriage, security. The desire for security is part of the woman's heart: they and their children, actual or to be born, must be secure. The question is, can touch do this, make a woman's heart run wild?

Men can answer this from experience by remembering the hearts of the past girls or women they touched. Remember the bonding that immediately took place. The simple request of Galatians 5:16 verifies that care should be taken when applying touch. But some Christian readers peculiarly want science to verify what they already know. For that, I recommend that you use your favorite search engine and ask, "What does science say about touch?" After your happy searching, you will find that science has now, after thousands of years, discovered that touch is powerful. For the human brain to know it is being touched, God has created cells, muscle, and nerves connecting the place touched to the brain or heart. Definite electrical, biological, and chemical reactions make all this take place. All are assessed and analyzed, creating question after question to our heart program, and the questions must be answered, creating a decision made at what seems to be the speed of light. Imagine yourself as small as the charge created on the skin and riding that charge throughout the human body until a decision is made. You would be on a wild ride! All this is happening when a woman is touched and leads to more decisions of the heart when she decides, "Yes, I am loved!"

What happens to the body when there is a sudden change of events, and she finds out that her understanding was wrong? What happens to a switch constantly being turned on and off? What happens when switches get warn out? This happens to men also in different ways and for different reasons. When he gets older, a man's questioning veers in a slightly different direction. Long-term security may not so important. Other questions must be taken into account and analyzed. It is easy to see how the heart program can become overused and worn out when wrong touch is fulfilled. Notice how our hearts grow less and less like the perfect heart we received from God when we were born. Notice how wear and tear affects the heart.

More responses to touch, truthfully already known, will be scientifically discovered in the future. More responses to touch will be discovered when touch takes place. But understand how intense the programs in her heart become when touch is involved. This program varies from person to person, depending on how often rejection enters the heart. And yes, as an electrical charge, touch can be a wild ride—similar, I would say, to a man or woman in battle … a battle for love.

# The Fragility of the
# Human Heart

*Humans are fragile creations.* Even powerful humans are so fragile they can be killed with a touch. I won't teach you how, but many people already know this. Christ has always known this. It is one reason the Creator, God of Abraham, whom we believe in, has always tried to promote love between God and neighbors.

The human heart is fragile and can be killed with a word. I don't know what words trigger you, but there was a vibrant young girl who lost some weight and looked good. Her boyfriend mentioned the word *fat*. Her heart was broken and dying. She immediately went on a crash diet and lost weight. She continued dieting until her life was threatened at a weight of under eighty pounds—a dangerous, life-threatening weight for the woman. Thankfully, God intervened and saved her life, but I wonder how many women die from anorexia, killed with a word. How many deaths occur by the repetitive misuse of other words?

How many words are misused against you? How many people are dying from the abuse of words?

Meditate on this a moment. I know you feel strong now, made bulletproof by attack after attack against your heart. But in reality, all you have is a heart full of holes. Yes, you have to defend yourself in the marketplace or outside in an unsafe world. But would you like to go home to a peaceful place? A place that is bullet-free, where you can lay down your arms?

The Bible says if you live by the sword, you will die by the sword. Could Jesus have been talking about the swords you choose to display in your home? Is it possible Jesus is teaching you how to have a place of rest, peace, and love in your home?

You can choose between two roads. You can forcefully demand "peace" without concern for the others in your house. But this road leads not to peace but to destruction—arguments, fighting, police, arrest, jail time, or divorce. Force must constantly be applied, and you have to check your back. Or you can learn what Job knew (Job 16:4). On that road, you know *words can be used to strengthen or weaken.* You can choose to be the High Priest and the example to your bride and maintain control of your tongue. Replace cursing with blessing. You can choose to strengthen your bride's heart by listening, searching, seeking, learning, and healing what is on it. Your bride, with her own fallen heart, will no longer have to wait for Christ's return to have an example of love to follow.

By simply accepting the fragility of your bride's heart, you can work toward creating a state of paradise in your house. Through your bride's heart, you can achieve heaven on earth, have a peaceful house, and not have to watch your back, using your words and actions to heal.

### God's Original Command

The original command by God for the human heart was for the groom to marry and love his bride completely, for life, all senses included. But the Old Testament reveals that after the Fall, *complete love* for life was such a problem that Adam and Eve could not have a functioning loving family, or even a family that would not kill each other. The problems are revealed throughout the Bible. Love for God, as well as love among groom and bride, brothers and sisters, and family, could not be created. From the beginning, God planned to offer a second solution. The Bible shows the answer was to restrain the powerful and troublesome touch program and provide the option for His human creations to wait to marry His Son, the Messiah, upon His return. That is what will satisfy your God-made original heart program—your quest for an equally perfect heart. A godly heart that wants and will love you.

I should explain more fully what I mean by your "heart program." You were very comfortable and satisfied with your mother holding you. If you were blessed for a time—and it might have been very short, depending on your circumstances—you enjoyed your mother's touch and presence. If you can see and hear, you may have enjoyed the sight and sounds of your mother. Some like being with their mother so much that they can't bear to part with her. It is a simple God-created program; many have been given a chance to love their mother's look, touch, and taste until their belly is full. Lust, perversion, and sin were not in your heart then. The terms *heterosexual, homosexual,* and *lesbian* imply sexual activity, which was not on your heart then. These and other sexual identities develop later, when the heart reacts to attacks against it, some sooner than others. Only you know exactly what these attacks against your heart are. Your heart was attacked with words against you, maybe improper touch, violent or nonviolent—only you know. You had to survive them.

You continued to grow, and your God-given beauty program kicked in. Some of you liked what you saw and were ready to share the love God programmed you to give. You probably hugged and kissed your father, mother, aunts, uncles, and cousins. If you were not abused, this was God-programmed love and not sexual. In your early stages of existence, you did not care about your parents' appearance. You were ready to love. When your beauty program started, you probably enjoyed it. You enjoyed and admired the beauty of the males and females in your family. If you were not abused, this was not sexual. Your parents then took you outside, and you began to meet other people. You might have been afraid, searching, wanting to fulfill God's love program. You met men, women, boys, and girls. Your beauty program was at work; you may have liked what you saw. You might've enjoyed the presence of different people, male or female. If you were not abused, your appreciations were not sexual. You just liked what you saw.

If you started playing as a toddler, you might have felt pressured to hang out with toddlers and children of the same sex. I understand. With married straight adults divorcing at a rate of 50 percent, you probably did not understand or get along with the opposite sex. It is possible the opposite sex threatened or scared you. They were weird. You might have been told to stay away from the girls or to leave them, the girls, alone. You may have continued trying to fulfill God's bonding program, making friends with children of your sex. You may have liked how they looked, felt more comfortable with them, and tried to become best buds.

You may have hugged, shaken hands, or high-fived when you were young. When you were young, you may have imitated sports figures and slapped the butts of kids like you, of your sex; you may have admired the physique of someone of your sex and wanted to be like them. I remember one young boy always looking at and admiring male weight lifters. You may have liked some other activity, such as ballet. Your culture may have favored dance, and maybe you started imitating gyrating to music promiscuously. But at that age, you probably did not know the word "promiscuous." You were simply using your God-given imitation program. Actions like these did not involve sexual thoughts in your heart.

And then *the change started, and all its problems.* As you started to get older, you learned new words. Abuse against you may have begun. All you wanted to do was fulfill your God-given heart program. With your mind like a magnet, you saw and heard bad words, expressions, attitudes, unloving ways of being, perversion, violence, foul arguments, disrespect, and maybe more. Perhaps these words were used against you—maybe repeatedly, sadly, and possibly even from your father or mother. Maybe your fragile young heart was told you were gay. That was abuse, an attack, and a lie. God did not make you that way.

You may have heard many other words and seen many different sinful actions; possibly, they were against you. You may not have been able to get godly direction; the sin may not have come from you, but it is a sinful world that your tiny heart had to process. You may have had to process it alone. You may have absorbed these wrong words, actions, expressions, and beliefs while they flowed and were used to abuse you.

You may not have received proper attention. Imagine little hearts without the example of a proper father or mother, how it can affect choices, actions, attitudes, and life. It may have affected your God-created original heart. Only you remember what happened to you. It could have happened in many ways. Maybe you were forced to sit in front of the TV—I consider that as potential abuse. It definitely changed your understanding of beauty from real beauty to fake, possibly creating false wants that in truth will not satisfy your God-given heart program. Perhaps your father did not notice that you were being fed false doctrines that led you to disrespect him. Your mother may not have known of the sins you were being forced to watch on the TV, computer, or phone—clearly a sin against your heart.

The sins against you continued as other people you met had their God-made heart programs warped. You may have been bullied. You may have been given addictive drugs. You may have only been able to hang out with the wrong crowd. You may have been taught the wrong things. You may have been touched in the wrong way. The sins of the tongue may have been used against your heart. You may have survived the first sin done against you.

What if multiple sins were committed against you? What if you were sinned against repeatedly?

In today's world, you quickly reached a time when you were offered material things. Some were necessary for you to live, such as food. Some seemed attractive to you, and you were programmed to touch them. At such an early stage, it might have been difficult to process how to deal with the materials you were given. If you indeed remember, you did not really want material things. Yes, your inquisitive heart was quick to grab items, and you played with them for a while. But your heart was truly made for God, or at least God's heart in a living, loving person. The things provided to you may have been confusing. They may have been shiny, pretty, furry, or colorful, but I firmly believe there was a time in your life when, if you were forced to choose, you would have preferred a living person. Why were so many of those material things you were given forgotten, ignored, left alone, and dropped on the floor? Why were you always pursuing your mother or the person raising you? You were made for people. Your little heart had to process this.

## A Lifetime to Go

Meditate on your mature self, the way you are now, and ask yourself: how many material things do you keep in the closet, basement, or attic? These are things you have chosen not to throw away, but in truth they are not necessarily a priority in your life. You have put them away. You leave out what you want to use and keep those things available. It is not that the things in your closet are bad or good. But the truth is, these things are not really important to you. Some you never use anymore. You may go through now and then and throw things away.

Have you ever thought about the real reason you have made these things less important to your life? The truth is, these are just things. They don't look at you, need you, want you, care about you, listen to you, say great things about you, or touch you. You know deep in your heart, as you once understood as a child, that there is no way you can get love from these unimportant things. You know deep in your heart not to give priority to things that won't love you.

So consider reawakening your true priorities. Give attention to what has a possibility of fulfilling the love you have always wanted, the love you have been searching for since you were born: your bride's heart. That is what Jesus is concerned about. Perhaps that is the "thing" you should be giving attention to, the thing you should be seeking, learning about, trying to understand, helping, caring for, feeding, listening to, talking to, touching, wanting, and loving. Your bride is a lifelong endeavor and should not to be put on the sidelines until your last heartbeat. *Her heart* is what you truly want and love.

# Original Sin and the
# Perfect Heart God Made

*All my life, I* have listed to pastors talking about sin, sin, sin.
It is hard for me to believe that people don't know what sin is.
It is on every channel, in almost every book, on the radio, and
indirectly even listed in the Bible. People have made lists of over
two thousand sins. Accusations of sin are made, righteously or
not, every day. I refuse to list them in my book. If you want a list,
feel free to seek elsewhere—I am sure you will find many who
want to point out your sins.

But not many people will tell you what original sin is. They tell
you how it occurred, with Adam eating the forbidden fruit and a
vague idea that men went from good to bad, but not much more.
Some say original sin never happened and does not exist. I disagree.
I will tell you what original sin is. It occurred when Adam and Eve
ate the fruit God told them not to eat. What happened? Suddenly
Adam's and Eve's perfect God-created hearts became filled with all
the sins people have listed. I trust these sins are fully revealed in the
Bible, but you will have to read the Bible to get the full list.

After the Fall, hearts became broken and confused with sin, no longer fully trusting and loving each other or God. For those who say original sin does not exist, for the pastors who say no one knows anymore what sin or original sin is, for people who are still curious, I ask this question: Have you noticed it is a sinful world out there? Have sins been committed against you? Use the rest of this page to write them out.

The sins you wrote down came from Adam. I say *Adam* because the Bible reveals that God held him responsible for them. Not Eve. I strongly believe if Adam had obeyed God, we would be living in a different world.

What happened to you comes from original sin. People demand a list of sins so they can make themselves righteous, but that desire can lead to other sins. Again, lists are available for those who want to search. But to simplify, I suggest you analyze the sins committed against you. Remember how they made you feel. How bad you felt because of them. How they have changed your original God-programmed perfect heart.

Now ask Jesus to help you forgive those who committed those sins against you, and ask the Holy Spirit to help you not repeat them yourself. You know they are bad; you are aware of the bad effects they had on your heart. You are experienced in the matter. Make the change not to repeat those sins yourself. Stop the spread.

I hope out of concern for your brothers you become somewhat familiar with the other forms of original sin. You now know what to do, so you can now help your brothers. Consider that most sins originate from a refusal to love. God's first two commandments explain them all.

Commandment 1: Love God.
Commandment 2: Love your neighbor.

Original sin came from outside the body to the inside via the fruit Adam and Eve ate, which directly changed their original God-programmed hearts from the perfect state they were made with. The Bible reveals our hearts as now divided, fractured, fallen, not always loving, not always feeling happy, not always feeling safe, not always feeling secure, not satisfied, not loving or in love as they once were—and that might not be a complete list of changes. Thanks to the devil's lack of knowledge. Adam's heart and Eve's were now, for all of God's purposes, dead. God had to start again. The Bible reveals all His efforts.

How did this original sin pass from Adam and Eve to their children? I was observing how we are today, and explaining that is easy. It passed through the senses. Not that the senses are bad; they are just the mechanism through which the good and bad pass to the heart—the eyes, ears, mouth, and touch.

It is not hard to understand how original sin passed from generation to generation. Though the devil's error might have been intentional, it is not hard to realize that not all original sin was intentionally passed from person to person.

Consider how you were treated when you were a baby, or later in your life. How did you react? First, your small heart could barely keep up with the data coming from the senses. What may have appeared to be a shock to you invariably is processed by God's primary program which includes those vital internal questions: does that person hear me, want to look at me, listen to me, want me, love me? You demanded godly love. Sin committed against you may have broken down your original God-created heart program over time.

I remember my first sin shock. I was a babe in a carriage; my mother, whom I had bonded with and loved, was pushing me around. My vision was not sharp yet, a little cloudy, black and white. Then another woman I did not recognize took over the carriage and pushed me away for many blocks. My God-created program turned on. The vital questions were asked. Would I see my mother again? Would she hear me again? Would she listen to me, want me, love me again? Being held—the sense of touch, proper touch reinforces love. *Shock, process, solution. Who is this? Scream loud, and let the tears flow. Don't give up. Cry block after block. Will somebody see me, hear me, want me, love me, bring me back to my mother, who I have bonded with and love?* What is a baby-sized processor (brain/heart) supposed to do? How do you expect a baby to analyze the situation?

After what seemed morally wrong, I was pushed into a strange room I had never seen before, and *smack!* My aunt struck me in the face. I didn't remember ever seeing her before. I learned I had an aunt the hard way. What do you think I thought when I returned to my mother? You don't know yet? I was thinking, *My mother sees me, hears me, listens to me again, wants me, and loves me.*

As you age, you may learn other words that reveal questions in your heart to analyze situations. Are all these questions always in you? Do you absorb and learn them as you grow? I don't know. I believe Adam and Eve were programmed with God's complete heart program, and after the Fall hit with every sin program in the Bible. These vital questions are good and often used by you. As you experience life, more may be added. Some of these questions you add are good, and some are sinful. Your heart seems to be constantly reacting to those basic internal questions.

As you meet new people, you constantly apply those questions that God programmed. I wonder how fast you are processing those questions inside you from the beginning, every time you meet someone. If you are single, meet someone, and are satisfied with the answer to those vital questions, you tend to stay with that person and be happy. If you are not, you may lose attention or even try to get away quickly. What if your baby, toddler, child, or teenager answers those internal questions incorrectly, as I did when I was in the carriage with my aunt?

Besides choosing to stay or run away, your heart decides to absorb or discard the "original" sin used against you. Many people and some religions don't believe in original sin. I heard a priest say children today don't know what sin is; they don't know the Ten Commandments. But ask these people to think back as far as they can—throughout all their years, back to the beginning. Ask them, "Did anyone do anything bad to you?"

Has anyone sinned against you?

Have you ever experienced what I would call a failure of authority?

I am sure many of you have profound, painful examples of bad things that have happened to you. They may have been big shocks to your heart or maybe many little assaults warping your heart over time. These were sins committed against you. The first time they were committed against you, undoubtedly they were "original" to you. Your heart may have been shocked. You also have a program that demands fairness. You may not have known this at the time, resulting in the imitation of sin committed against you. Know now that God responds to those who sinned against you by promising, "Vengeance is mine" (Deuteronomy 32:35 NKJV).

My heart, and at one time your heart, demanded to be present, close, and experience the presence and heart of God with every person met. We are programmed to expect and demand God's heart from sinners, no matter the condition of our hearts. With such demands of love programmed into our hearts from the beginning, it becomes understandable that we go through life like battling tops in a tight space (Jeremiah 17:9–10).

I don't know what you went through in your life, but it is easy for me to understand why you are the way you are. Each person is different. Some sin experienced is small, quickly processed, and overcome. But there are people whose hearts had to process sin after sin against them. Many minor sins against them every day. Sins spoken by the tongue. Other people have had to process big sins against their hearts. The wages of sin are death. *You might be dying.*

Think of the sins used against you. Since birth, your heart has been like a magnetic sponge attracting and absorbing everything you experience. Have you absorbed and chosen to repeat those sins? Do you notice a difficulty existing in the world because of those sins you repeat? Problems in your job, family, marriage, lifestyle, or health result from those sins you absorbed.

Many Christian men say you should not judge the heart, but I have just revealed that you have been judging hearts all your life from the day you were born. Some have survived and overcome, and many have not. I have found that Christ is the only way to overcome sins against my heart—seeking, listening, learning from, talking to, obeying Him. Awakening to the saving price He paid for my sin as well as sins against me. Awakening to the price He paid for the sins against my heart. I have found freedom in knowing that the debt is paid and I am forgiven, in knowing that my heart is forgiven, complete, whole, wanted, appreciated, loved once and for all. I read the scriptures and realize that He sent a living Helper to guide me, heal me, teach me how to love, verifying what is in the scriptures. Through Jesus I can see I am loved. And I believe the same is required for your heart.

With your new born-again self, with your healed, whole, complete, and no longer fractured heart, you can now see clearly the true hearts of others, knowing what Jesus knows about the heart. You can take responsibility and help other hearts in need, possibly your bride's. You can be the high priest in your house, setting the proper loving example with Christ and the Holy Spirit's help.

## God Will Avenge You

Meditate on this: I was walking on the boulevard with a family member. During the walk, we saw a young, beautiful girl, about twenty-two years old, sitting on the sidewalk, her head slightly tilted down, wearing no shoes, with a cup in front of her to beg for money.

The family member I was walking with said, "She looks able. Why does she not get a job?"

"You don't know the sins committed against her in her lifetime," I said. "You don't know her story. You don't know what happened to *her heart*."

Each person has a story. You know yours, and only you know how bad the sins against you were. Have you ever considered the sins committed against the people who sinned against you? Have you ever wondered what *their* story is? Again I ask you to consider choosing not to absorb and repeat those sins committed against you.

Jesus knows all hearts. He designed and created them, and built yours. He knows what was done against you. Jesus promises vengeance when He spoke of the millstone (Luke 17:2 KJV). Consider doing your best to let Jesus handle the sins committed against you. Jesus understands why you repeated the sin, and He died on the cross to pay the price to forgive all sins, including yours. He is willing to forgive you, help you, and heal you. Why don't you ask Him?

Because of Adam, there is sin in the world, passed from person to person via the senses—I believe mainly through the eyes and ears.

Yet your heart constantly asks those vital questions each time someone sins against you. With your God-given moral code and the heart of a baby, toddler, or child, you had to process and judge each time you were sinned against. Some of you might have quickly lost your paradisial state of heart because of your parents or family. If you survived that, you had to process the sins of friends, acquaintances, schools, churches, authority figures, computers, phones, TV, theaters, magazines, radio, bosses, work acquaintances, strangers, customers, neighbors, and spouses. And what books have you been reading?

At the time, you may not recognize sins made in your presence as attacks against your heart. Jesus is the way to that perfect heart of God you are looking for. He wants to return you to paradise.

# From "You" to "I"

*Have you made it* back to *you* yet? A time in your life existed when all you wanted to do was fulfill your God-given heart program to love and be loved, but it was bugged, warped, and erased a little every day. This battering may continue even today. Do you still have that original heart program God gave you?

To understand, you have to go back to the book of Genesis, before the Fall of Adam. What was life like? After the Fall, Adam became like us. Like we are now. You may know that program if you have been living long enough. But before Adam's fall, God created Adam and Eve and said that it was *good*. What was good? There was much love, beauty, understanding, appreciation, happiness, joy, peace, satisfaction, care, and light work. The senses were good before Adam and Eve ate the forbidden fruit. God had no concerns or complaints about Adam and Eve living life naked in the garden as long as they had their original, God-created, innocent, and undivided hearts. But before the Fall of Adam, there was something else.

For over two thousand years, men and women have prayed, worshiped, praised, loved, talked, gathered, remembered, and walked with God in the belief that He is the most important Person in existence—and I agree. I believe God is most important, and at the same time the Bible shows that from the beginning, God the Father, the Son, and the Holy Spirit have been in a heart state of "you." God the Father commanded us to love Him, desires obedience, and wants to be remembered and given attention, but the biblical and historical record reveals just as clearly that the God of Abraham treats His human creation as most important. The Father wants a kingdom, but that is the last thing of importance on His list.

Awaken to all the things our Father created for us first. He continued His provision for person after person, kingdom of men after kingdom of men, expecting to see love for Him and for neighbor, love between bride and groom. The Bible reveals that each person failed, except for three or four going to heaven(depending on what version of the Bible you use). The Son Jesus proved that your life is more important to Him than His. The Holy Spirit is creating realities for your heart first. With that understanding, you might come to realize that in the garden before the Fall, all three hearts—of our Father, Adam, and Eve—were in a perfect state of "you."

In the garden before Adam's fall, God was appreciated and worshiped, but at that time each heart was operating perfectly, programmed for one another like this:

> I love you.
> What you want is most important to me.
> I love you so much that I often ask, "What can I do for you?"
> I am here to serve you!

With hearts in a state of "you," all were served and loved, and the God-created heart program was satisfied. All were at peace, without fear, stress, or needing to process those five vital internal questions:

1. Will you look at me and see me?
2. Will you hear me?
3. Will you listen to me?
4. Will you want me, do you want me?
5. Will you, do you love me? Will you be close to me?

The touch program, the being close, answers the question, "Are you really there?" God is amazing! I believe.

## A Heart in a State of "You"

Jesus teaches us to have a heart in a state of "you." The "you" program is the state of heart that exists in paradise. It is the love program, which satisfies those vital internal questions and solidifies your important created desire to love, which God put in you. These two programs—a desire to want an equal/opposite godlike person with God's original undivided heart, and to be wanted by that person (love)—is what makes us different from the angels, and definitely different from the demons.

At birth, we are perfectly programmed by God, wanting to be wanted and wanting to love. This program is processed through the senses. This heart program is so pure the babe does not even care if the mother or father they bond with is beautiful or ugly, young or old. The child does not want to be alone—and isn't that you, at least once in your life?

I once heard a pastor say that God could order a single angel into the darkness of deep space, alone in an Apollo space capsule, for five thousand years without contact from God or anyone else. The pastor said the angel would stay there obediently and faithfully without complaint or contact until God returned. Humans are made different; many don't survive solitary confinement for long without damaging their hearts and souls.

As a babe, your heart was born with a strong desire to use your senses to give love and receive love. Some annoyed parents claim you were sinful when you were a baby because you screamed so loud. But you just wanted to love and be loved—you were in pain, or your diapers needed changing, and you did not know what to do. You just wanted to be loved. Same when you were hungry, thirsty, tired, or needing to be burped. Then when those simple things were satisfied, you wanted to look at, listen to, talk to, touch, want, and love the person you bonded to.

That is how God made you; that is what you knew how to do. That was your original God-created perfect state of heart—a moral heart, until you were sinned against. Your fall is similar to Adam's in that sin entered your heart from outside. Adam and Eve fell after eating the forbidden fruit; from outside, all sin entered their hearts. I believe they were in shock. Their Paradise-original, God-programmed heart changed from a state of "you" to "I." The new question in their hearts was, *What about me?* The "I" became most important. All the world tells you "I" is most important. Look outside! How is that working for men, women, and children worldwide?

# Equal/Opposite

*"Love" is the easy* answer to the question of purpose. I am sure you can think of other purposes for marrying your bride. It is essential to understand that the love desires God programmed into Adam and Eve from the beginning were warped after the Fall. For many couples following Adam and Eve, love is forgotten after the Fall. The original sins against a couple before marriage and continuation of sins against each other after the marriage will lead to the breakdown of the marriage.

The roles of Adam and Eve are defined in scripture with the word "helper" describing Eve. But what does that mean? The definitions of "helper" and "head of household" are changed and weakened with each sin. The word "helper" has confounded many church leaders, governments, men, women, grooms, and brides across the generations. Many people use it as a fighting word—the devil is happy about that. Efforts to define "helper" other than what is used in the Bible have been less than sufficient. However, many men today consider "helpers" as being on a lower level than those being helped or secondary to them. I beg to differ. This opinion reflects the reality that many helpers were mistreated or poorly treated over the centuries, and therefore regarded as "lesser." The exciting thing is that many centuries after God created the word "helper," history also tells what the ultimate helper is.

Imagine yourself as a high person of rank, a president. It does not matter what you are president of—it could be a company, a country, even president of the United States. You could be in charge of a battalion. As a head, there are things that you know from experience are right. These decisions can be made; these decisions are you. They are accurate, and you may not need help on what you don't need help on. What about decisions you need to make that you are unsure of, things you are not capable of handling, burdens you cannot shoulder?

Leaders need to surround themselves with helpers. History shows that leaders and presidents surround themselves with basically two types of helpers, to oversimplify it: people who are "yes" people, and helpers willing to offer their "differing opinions." Too many people in charge, *even presidents*, have surrounded themselves with yes-men. Though it might be more comfortable and work for a while, we can observe that not receiving functional, differing, true, and trustworthy opinions has led to the downfall of many a president or leader. Leaders should know to appreciate the helpers they have chosen to trust. Yes-men may be needed sometimes, but often you will need an honest and differing opinion you can trust. So treat your helpers well.

To varying degrees, God has made and offers you the same in the heart of your bride—your helper. A helper's role may fall somewhere within a range of agreeing, differing. God has given you the final say—the *responsibility*—but loving your helper well will get your marriage through challenges your family may encounter. Some brides won't say a word, and yes may be their only answer. Other brides let their opinions, observations, and conclusions flow freely. Most are in-between. There are many reasons for her to be the way she is. The reasons ultimately leads to *her heart*. You have chosen someone to love and will have to work, deal, and be with for life.

Ideally, you will have assessed the abilities and knowledge of yourself and of your bride and helper *before* marriage. Decide before you marry because after marrying it may be too late—God offers you no opportunity for divorce. If you take the part, you must take the whole bride.

In my previous book, *How to Pick Your Bride and How to Keep Her for Life*, I recommended that before marriage, the groom should make lists. Lists of what he wants, lists of what she wants—lists to find out whether you and your bride are equally yoked. You can add to that a list which contains a true analysis and understanding of your bride's abilities and capabilities. In my first book, I wrote of this as "the wonders she can do." I believe this is the true meaning of what God meant when He said Adam "knew" Eve—a knowing that includes the mental as well as the physical, but also *the heart*. Appreciate the wonders she can do! Realize that her opinions may be good. God made her that way. Applying what she knows to what you know as a leader in your family decisions clearly multiplies the family's capabilities. Your bride's capability and opinions, wisely considered, are a sign of good leadership. Does God listen to you?

Why listen? It could be wise for you, as head of household, to seek advice from your bride. Let's say you are a top lawyer in your city, and your bride is a leading orthopedic doctor. Wouldn't it be beneficial to heed her advice if you break a bone mowing the lawn? Though the abilities of groom and bride can vary wildly, your smart decisions, like those of any businessman or manager with access to employees, should take into account and appreciate what your bride knows and can do. She is the most crucial living gift God has given you.

Though ultimately the Father, Jesus, and the Holy Spirit are the only persons who can truly save our lives, God has brought many people into our lives in the process of saving us.

Many people in this country have had their lives saved by other people. If you allow yourself, you might remember times in your life when your bride saved you. Maybe one evening when you worked all day without a meal and were ready to starve to death, you came home to your Bride's tasty home-cooked meal. I am sure you can find other examples—like the broken bone above—when your bride saved you and gave to you, if you think about it. And isn't "save" an important word? Is *the one who saves you* important?

## Ezer Kenegdo

Since many families are confused by today's mostly incorrect definition of the word "helper" as being the purpose of a bride, maybe the original word used by God in the Old Testament (Torah) will explain much. Ask this question of the Messiah.

In Genesis 2:18, the Lord God revealed the program and said, "It is not good for the man to be alone; I will make him a helper suitable for him." In the Torah, the word for "helper" is *ezer kenegdo*, used also in Genesis 2:20. Genesis 2:23 contextually implies Eve has fulfilled this role—that is, she is essential. *Ezer* means both "help" and "save." I wonder if God's use of the word *ezer* in two different ways in the Torah hints that there may be times in your life when your bride will have to save you. We know God is the one who saves, but I believe He is encouraging men and women to save lives in different ways. *Ezer* (help) seems to be a high-ranking word many don't appreciate today in this spoiled world. God is the Creator and Savior, but every person in the garden—God, Adam, and Eve, is supposed to save the others from loneliness, boredom, and lack of love.

More important to me, because it explains so much, is the word *ke*, which means "like," and *neg*, which means "opposite." *Keneg* ("like/opposite") explains the physical body and heart program God put into Adam and Eve before the Fall, giving them strong desire and love for each other. When they ate the forbidden fruit, these programs were attacked (as with a virus), requiring intervention by God. When babies mature during their life, God invigorates their *keneg* program by the maturation of their reproductive systems. Sadly, because of sins against them in their lifetime, some never reach a mature state of heart to accept this program.

*Ke* also verifies the importance of the helper, Eve—your bride. Eve was made from Adam's side, with *ke* ("like") implying the equality. You are in charge of her in having the final say and being responsible, but Christ teaches you to lead by example as chief of servants in your household. *Ke* also verifies physical sameness: the same two eyes, two hands, two ears, two arms, two legs, two feet, one nose, one mouth. Eve is human, the same as Adam and just like him—virtually equal. They rank as equally crucial in God's eyes: "in His own image, in the image of God He created man; male and female He created them" (Genesis 1:27, Inductive Study Bible NASB).

God will listen to your prayer and your bride's equally. What could be more equalizing than praying to God, whose image you are made from, backed by His promise to hear and answer your prayers? Adam said, "Bone of my bone and flesh of my flesh"— equally liked, wanted, and loved.

Some men try to avoid the strong and undeniable desire God created in them for an equal and opposite bride to their sadness, disappointment, and possibly their demise. These God-created programs will always be included in the wants of your heart.

The *neg* element of *ezer kenegdo* means "opposite." It is that small but powerful and now necessary 1 percent difference, the physical opposite of Adam—your bride and all that entails, including the genitalia and their system for reproduction. The *neg*, the equal and opposite program, explains the success of many marriages issuing from the doubled and different strengths distributed between the bride and the groom. When these different strengths are not used maturely in the union, it reveals and results in marital problems.

Understanding how equal and opposite you are to a potential bride before marriage would be helpful. "Equal and opposite" includes the physical but also the mind and the heart. To what extent do you need to be equal with your bride? To what extent does she need to be equal? The opposite will also be there, so consider these questions.

- Are there personality opposites?
- Is there a female way of thinking and a male way of thinking or observing?
- Are there differences as to what is essential?
- Are there family or cultural differences?
- Are there different abilities?
- Is there a stronger need to feel secure in her heart?

I believe God put different parts of His heart in your bride than He may have in yours. Your bride's knowledge, opinions, understanding, and observations may be more different than you realize for the glory of God. How much of her opposite heart can you deal with? Are you mature enough to deal with that difference wisely?

In my previous book, I explained the mature Christlike way to deal with your bride, with an "equally yoked" section to guide you toward a balanced marriage. But God made your bride for many reasons. Giving you a differing point of view is the purpose I wish to emphasize here. A complementary opposite is necessary for even the most essential high-level persons in this world. It is part of the program God made to create life as we know it. It will be up to you to know how much opposition is needed to maintain the safe existence of yourself and your family in this temporary world.

God is the highest example I can give you of a Person willing to listen and communicate with His helper. Note that God needs no help, but He freely chooses to listen, as He does to Moses and as He freely chooses to listen to you when He says, "Ask and keep on asking." It is essential to deal with the opposites in your bride maturely.

In your bride's physical body, soul, and spirit, which includes *her heart*, God has given you enough in life to love, to fight loneliness, and to be not bored. There is much to know about God and your bride. God may also give you children; if not, there are friends; if not, there are people in need. In truth, God considers the rest of the materials on this earth unimportant. Even gold, the precious metal many men worship, God seems to consider worthy only to put under the feet of those who enter His city. In the vision of Revelation 21:21 (NIV), "The twelve gates were twelve pearls, each gate made of a single pearl. The great street of the city was of gold, as pure as transparent glass." Material things are a great gift from God, but notice how the great gift of gold is not life-giving but only meant to walk on. The real gift we should be paying attention to is God Himself and the Bride. It is what we truly and always will want—someone alive who loves and wants us.

The Bible reveals that God took action and time, planning to ensure that even Adam and Eve could not resist each other. God does the same to help you and your bride fight the conflict and confusion between the "you" and the "I" switching on and off in your heart. Has your marriage returned to the "you" program yet? It has to start with *you*!

## The Fight for the Love of Her

With their new sinful nature, God had to throw Adam and Eve out of the garden. Their hearts became just like ours, battling between love and hate as you and I do.

If you watch the news, you can watch the effects of the original sin program. You can see what we humans are now capable of, both good and bad. The immediate effect is seen in the Old

Testament in the story of Cane and Abel (Genesis 4:8). Before the Fall, there was no desire for killing among God, Adam, and Eve. There was a breakdown in the heart after the Fall. You can see the breakdown of the hearts of men in the Bible, history books, and the news. Murder and other sins against you continue until this day. Awaken to the repairs to the heart God made immediately after the Fall in Genesis.

God has been fighting the original sin program since the Fall. God is in the fight for the love of *her,* your bride. Scripture reveals that God knew beforehand that Adam and Eve would fall. He knew if they ate the fruit they would die. The hearts would no longer know what love is. He added critical things to their heart program.

After eating the fruit, Adam and Eve found that their bodies were changed to deal with life after the Fall. Genesis 3:7 (International Inductive Study Bible) says: "Then the eyes of both of them were opened, knew they were naked." The eyes work very fast, as does the process. Suddenly, after they ate the forbidden fruit, they knew they were naked. They did not know this before. Here is the passage (Genesis 3:7–9) in five versions.-

> And the eyes of them both were opened, and they knew that they were naked; and they sewed fig leaves together, and made themselves aprons. And they heard the voice of the LORD God walking in the garden in the cool of the day: and Adam and his wife hid themselves from the presence of the LORD God amongst the trees of the garden. And the LORD God called unto Adam, and said unto him, Where art thou? (KJV)

> Suddenly their eyes were opened to a reality previously unknown. For the first time, they sensed their vulnerability and rushed to hide

their naked bodies, stitching fig leaves into crude loincloths. Then they heard the sound of the Eternal God walking in the cool misting shadows of the garden. The man and his wife took cover among the trees and hid from the Eternal God. God *(calling to Adam)*: Where are you? (The Voice)

And as they ate it, suddenly they became aware of their nakedness, and were embarrassed. So they strung fig leaves together to cover themselves around the hips. That evening they heard the sound of the Lord God walking in the garden; and they hid themselves among the trees. The Lord God called to Adam, "Why are you hiding?" (The Living Bible)

Immediately the two of them did "see what's really going on"—saw themselves naked! They sewed fig leaves together as makeshift clothes for themselves. When they heard the sound of God strolling in the garden in the evening breeze, the Man and his Wife hid in the trees of the garden, hid from God. God called to the Man: "Where are you?" (The Message)

Then the eyes of both were opened, and they knew that they were naked; and they sewed fig leaves together and made themselves aprons. And they heard the sound of the LORD God walking in the garden in the cool of the day, and the man and his wife hid themselves from the presence of the LORD God among the trees of the garden. But the LORD God called to the man, and said to him, "Where are you?" (RSVCE)

For further study, consider transliterated versions from Aramaic, Hebrew, and Greek.

Before they ate the fruit, genitalia, as adults have now, was not God's initial priority. Whatever the change was, it hints at a sudden, shocking, mental, and what appeared to them as a *physical* body change as soon as they ate the fruit.

Was there a physical change? One physical change occurred with their eyes; God made that happen when they ate the fruit. Were their eyes opening a programming or hardwiring change, as in the nerves or blood vessels? Did this change affect their hearts? Could their reproductive system mature and become fully functional so much more quickly than ours do when we enter puberty? Their reproductive process became what we have now as mature adults, or at least they suddenly noticed it. It was a definite change from their point of view and, I believe, a shock to them. Their eyes opened, and they were embarrassed. What was God doing?

The hearts of Adam and Eve were now in what seemed to be an ever-changing state of "I" and "you." Which is more important? *Both* now, with solid selfish tendencies—like many of us who so often argue and battle. Some of you may understand. You may have experienced this in your family or your life.

Did God change the form and application of genitalia? They are not formed by chance. Their purpose is to ensure that no matter how selfish Adam became; no matter how much he separated from Eve in farming, gathering, and exploring; no matter how angry he became, he would have to come back and assume a position that put Eve in front of his eyes so he could see who was *most* important.

God added a different program to Eve. No matter how peculiar Adam became, no matter the situation or how selfish he became, no matter how annoyed she was with Adam, her *desire* would be for her husband—but as a result of the Fall, they both forgot how to love. God chose to solve it this way: He commanded Eve to obey, and He commanded Adam to love. The scriptures reveal God's long, persistent efforts to teach men to love. The Bible tells of God's effort to bring groom and bride together. And with it all, God kept the original heart program that only God can fulfill: an internal, insatiable desire for God's heart.

# Judging the Heart

*In this chapter, we* turn to judging the heart—your own and hers. If the word "judge" sounds too final because of sins against you, replace that with a word such as "understand" or "discern."

First, judge yourself, and decide whether what I have written about the heart applies to you. Does it make sense to you? It may be that you now realize God started you with a perfect heart, one He made and deemed perfect. I say perfect because I am amazed by God's creations and believe the original hearts God created in the beginning once contained Gods laws. The original hearts God once created He said were good. The hearts God created are certainly better than the resulting ones formed by attacks of original sin. Recall the attacks against your heart over your years of life. Ask yourself, "Did I survive the attacks?" You will know after answering the following question: "Do I still want to be wanted?"

If you said yes, it is likely that your heart still has a pulse and wants to be alive.

Again recall the sins against you. Did you absorb any of them? Realize that on the cross, Jesus said, *"Tetelestai,"* which translates

39

to "it is finished," used by businesses and people in Jesus's time to refer to a bill, in the sense of "the debt is paid." Jesus offers to pay all debts (sins) in your life. He has paid for all of it! The evidence that it has been paid is that our Heavenly Father raised Jesus from the dead. Among the many Christian denominations, you will have to seek the path you want to take toward finding the forgiveness of Jesus. You might have seen Him alive or know Him by dreams and visions. You can simply have faith by reading, hearing from others who have been taught about Him, seen Him alive, and then believing.

Judge her heart in the same way.

In Matthew 7:4, Jesus tells you "to get the plank out of your own eye" before you can attempt to fix the hearts of others. One hinted Jesus will accept you as you are and make you clean. Who is the One? Jesus when He saved the thief on the cross. Come to Jesus! The thief on the cross considered Jesus as not guilty and asked Him to remember him when Jesus came to His Kingdom. Some may say how convenient to choose this path but consider the lost, wasted, lonely, dead and loveless life of the thief on the cross. He never had the chance to truly experience the love that God offers you while living on earth. Instead all he got was things, loneliness, pain and suffering. Other Christians say you should repent of your sin and ask Jesus to become your Savior—ask Him to come into your heart. Other Christian denominations say that more than this is needed. In Acts 4:12 (NIV) Peter said, "Salvation is found in no one else, for there is no other name under heaven given to mankind by which we must be saved."

I know there have been sins against your and your bride's perfect, God-created, God-given hearts, affecting your relationship with God, your eternal life, and life on earth. It perhaps is affecting your relationship with the people you meet, your present life situation, your health, and your family as well as each other. It is probably best to deal first with those sins committed against your own heart. Seek; find a way not to repeat sins committed against you upon someone else.

What do I believe? The way that has helped me is belief and faith in Jesus, along with faith in the Father and faith in the Holy Spirit; seeking the Creator, His Bible, and Christ's church; faith to pray often to our Father, Jesus, and the Holy Spirit; and learning from the good examples of people in my life. You may have found others.

Consider asking God in prayer to guide you. It might take years to work out the sins committed against you. Become *alive* and be aware of attacks against your heart. Once you have removed the plank from your own eye, you can see clearly to remove the speck from your brother's eye (Matthew 7:3–5),

Consider carefully *discerning* the heart of your bride: realize the way you judge others—including your bride—is the way God will judge you.

Consider what God told judges to do:

> Do not show partiality in judging; hear both small and great alike." You are recommended to bring any case too hard for you to God. (Deuteronomy 1:17 NIV)

> Consider carefully what you do; because you are not judging for man but for the Lord. (2 Chronicles 19:6 NIV)

Proverbs 24:23 seems to be saying not to show partiality.

With fairness you must judge. Sometimes you have to judge. Is she a good fit for you before marrying? You have to judge when there is an emergency in your marriage. You are supposed to judge and respond if her life is at stake. There are many times you have to judge. There are essential things you have to judge, but John 7:24 recommends stopping judging by mere appearance.

Do you have to judge everything she does while she is your bride? Every unimportant, unnecessary detail? Have you ever had a management position? Owned a company? What is the mindset of men in big business who manage every single small detail of each person who works in their companies? Have you ever worked under a person who micromanaged you?

"Do not judge, or you too will be judged" (Matthew 7:1 NIV). You have to decide wisely when to make a judgment, and then judge wisely. Many times judgment is not necessary; in marriage, grace and love are always essential. There also seems to be a response program built into the heart. Luke 6:37 (NIV) says, "Do not judge, and you will not be judged. Do not condemn, and you will not be condemned." If you choose to have a forgiving nature, you will be forgiven. This is not just Jesus talking. Have you noticed that when you become overly and unnecessarily judgmental against some person, they happily return the favor?

So how do you judge?

Sometimes, it seems as though "judge" is the correct word, but many hear the word and think of the final judgment that should be left to Jesus. If you are hesitant about the word, use "discern." God made us to exercise judgment in many situations and in regard to people and things. Am I providing enough food for my family? Are my bride and (later) my children OK? As we walk together, are we headed for trouble? Is my bride in need of something? Will my bride be warm enough in that coat I just purchased for her? Is my wife wearing her safety belt?

The scriptures reveal *God judges those He loves*. It is important to brake down that statement carefully. Note those whom God judges He first must love. I believe the scriptures reveal the love God has given to all people. It also reveals a hint: to be an effective judge on someone they first must believe, realize and know you love them.

When judging your bride, it is important to know that *her heart* started out like yours, made by God perfect, wanting to be wanted and loved. Sin came into her life and attacked her heart as it did yours. The sins attacking her heart may have been different from those attacking yours. Hopefully, you will be more forgiving, patient, empathetic, and understanding, and apply all the teaching from Jesus that I am sharing. Making an effort to know her heart and to notice and learn the sins committed against her is good judging. Decide whether you can accept and deal with those sins for life before you get married.

If you have removed your plank and chosen to marry her, you may think of her as the better half of the marriage. All is well. If that is not the situation, and you realize that like you, she has been sinned against, you may choose to begin the slow process of helping her rid herself of choosing the sin. There is only one way to solve your observed and judged problems. You have to offer her Christlike love consistently. Be a Christlike example with persistent Christlike care and understanding. It is the only way to fix *her heart.* Such methods are taught in the Bible (and also in my book *How to Pick your Bride and How to Keep Her for Life*).

Since you now know how to judge, you can patiently and quietly evaluate your bride's progress, teaching her by your example. With prayer and Bible study, the same way she absorbed the sins of others, she will appreciate and bond to your Christlike example as a loving, understanding assessor of *her heart.*

Slowly and patiently, with Christlike concern, seek and find out the sins committed against *her heart.* The sins might be recent or from a long time ago. Are there holes in her heart? Who is putting them there? Is it you? What effort have you made to patch up those holes? What is her heart searching for? Can you rebuild that heart with love? If you are persistent and consistent, and if you are caring, maybe she will wake up and ask you the question I have taught you to ask without fear. The question is what God asks you: "What do you want?"

### How to Judge Your Progress

In judging your own progress, notice even minor signs.

> Does she depend on you more?
>
> Is she talking to you more? Is she beginning to imitate your Christlike ways?
>
> Does she seek your attention more?
>
> Does she need to tell you how her day went more than she needs to tell her girlfriends?
>
> Is she trying to show more love to you the way she knows?
>
> Is she testing out her godlikeness by offering you choices between this and that?
>
> Does she seem to be bonding with you more?
>
> Does she seem to become more like Christ with you but does not have the confidence to say outright, "What do you want?"
>
> Do you have the godlike confidence to ask her that question?
>
> Do you know how to judge *her heart* now?
>
> Do you understand your bride's heart?
>
> Will you work hard to develop the patience and forgiveness of Christ in your marriage with her?
>
> Do you know the proper way to fix it?

The answer is *grace.*

If you are not seeing progress, if your answers are no, if she doesn't wake up and become alive and return original God-created perfect-hearted love to you immediately, I ask you to be patient just as Christ is patient with you. Keep trying. Don't give up. It is hard work you are doing, but God says the worker deserves his wages. Jesus has not forgotten you and promises you the reward of heaven. The reward is real!

# Praying with Your Bride

*It is important to* pray with your bride, creating a habit of consistent prayer together so that God can provide a chance for all to hear and know what is wanted. God wants to know, you want to know, and your bride wants to know. Set the example and lead in prayer. Consistency and persistence is the key.

Once the example is set, and your bride is confident in you and knows you are serious, encourage her to join in. If you have ears to hear, listen to her words carefully. Let your bride know she can ask God for anything, even if it is something against you. Don't respond in kind; don't attack back. Don't discuss it there. Her words are to be pondered over and carefully considered—something to ask God about in private. Be a man and learn what is on her heart. You might be able to provide something she needs or wants, but in ordinary conversation don't ask.

Praying out loud in your home with your bride is God's way for all to know one another. If your bride is not paying much attention to the praying, remain intent on knowing what is going on. If you have not been praying with your bride, you are missing out on one of God's greatest methods to keep a family together. So start praying. Require it in your household. Start slow and keep it light in the beginning. Build trust. Write down all the wants. Start leading your way deeper. Just as God listens for and to your prayers, listen carefully to your bride's prayers. —Create a positive prayer environment in your home. Listening sympathetically to your bride's prayers helps you know *her heart* in the way that God does.

My favorite prayer is the Lord's Prayer. I use the version found in Matthew 6: 9–13 (NIV).

> Our Father in heaven,
> hallowed be your name,
> your kingdom come,
> your will be done,
> on earth as it is in heaven.
> Give us today our daily bread.
> And forgive us our debts,
> as we also have forgiven our debtors.
> And lead us not into temptation,
> but deliver us from the evil one.

In my life, I have found it to be the most powerful prayer. But for many decades I prayed it over and over without really knowing what I was saying. Then one day, the Holy Spirit explained it to me, and I wrote it down as follows.

> My Father,
> Your Father,
> Our Father …

No matter what color, shape, and size, and no matter what you believe, through Jesus we all have access to our Father. The Father says to ask Him anything.

Who art in Heaven ...

Yes, He is up there, but He is also down here in your hearts—a part of Him was put there from the beginning, in the original God-programmed heart for the first man and first woman, and remains part of your heart today. Can you find it?

I believe that is what Jesus was talking about when he said to hold your lamp high to be seen.

Hallowed be Thy Name,

May it be set apart. We set Him apart; He is love, the guide on love to us. The love who loves us. If you have broken one commandment, you have broken them all. Sometimes you don't know what to do, so it is good to ask your Father, the one whose name you hallow. What love rules have you broken?

Forgive us Father, forgive us all.

Thanks to Jesus we now have access to the loving forgiveness of the Father.

In Jesus' name, I ask.

Thy Kingdom come ...

It is a future kingdom where love reigns. Do you want it?

Look at the kingdoms of the past. Look at your kingdom today. Are you satisfied with it? Does it make you feel comfortable? Does it make you feel safe?

I want the Father's kingdom to come; do you? I want love to reign; do you? Have you been seeking it out? Trying to make it happen? What about in your marriage?

If you agree with the Father, bringing His kingdom into reality, also ask Him for help getting your small kingdom—your family—to a heavenly reality. Seek His guidance on how by reading the Bible, His Word, and by prayer. Note His examples.

Thy will be done …

What is the Father's will? It is in His commandments: Love God, and love your neighbor. How have you been doing with that? Seek, search, find, and notice that fulfilling His will solidifies and helps your marriage and family.

On earth as it is in heaven.

I want that; do you? Not just on earth—in your family on earth. He tells you how to do it, and it starts with your heart.

Give us this day our daily bread.

Yes, feed us, Lord. Feed me and teach me to feed my wife and family both physically and spiritually. Food for the body. Physical food. Food for the soul. Food for the heart—spiritual food. Thank you, Father.

Forgive our trespasses, debts, as we forgive those who trespass against us.

Did you understand those words? Have you been a forgiving person? Have you mastered your ability to forgive? Do you want to be forgiven? Is there something you want to be forgiven for? Lord, forgive me and teach me to be forgiving. Jesus paid the debt. Believe in Him.

Lead us not into temptation …

Yes, Lord, I have been tempted enough. Have you? Have you ever tempted your brothers or sisters?

Father, I agree I don't want to be tempted; teach me to not become a tempter in my dealings with my bride.

But deliver us from evil.

Yes, all evil. The evil in the world is out there; have you seen it? The evil is all around me. Have you experienced it? The evil is in us. Yes, that is in there also in our hearts, possibly in our souls. It is not your fault. It came in when Adam and Eve committed the first sin. It has been passed along ever since, sneaking in through the senses—the eyes, the ears, the other senses, passing from generation to generation.

The senses are not bad; it is how love passes through. The problem is that when original sin passes through, it can be engulfing, ruining your heart and the hearts of the people around you. You just have to be aware, relearn what your sin is. and choose to not pass it on.

Have you been having trouble? Don't give up! Keep learning from the Father, the Son, and the Holy Spirit. Seek and knock. Pray and ask them for help.

Thank you, Father, for delivering men from evil and helping me to control the evil side of my heart, which is in me, so I don't expose it to my bride and family. Help me to keep alive my original God-created perfect heart.

Amen.

I believe; I agree. I will let you choose which to adopt.

Now read that prayer again because Christ's prayer is perfect for married couples; it reveals much.

Remember when you pray aloud with your bride to listen to what is on her heart. In the beginning of your learning to pray together, do not include concerns you have against your bride. Focus on what is on your heart: fears, things you want and need from God, things you feel should happen, situations your feel need to occur. Learn what is on her heart, and ask God to grant it?

When it comes time, include your children and what is on their hearts what they want God to grant. Ask God in front of her, for her and them. It does not matter if what you ask for is small or big; you just need to be listening and remembering.

Write the requests you hear in a book. Don't forget to praise and give thanks to God for answered prayers. Check them off in your book. Your consistent prayer together will bring you and your bride closer. If you can achieve free open prayer together among God, yourself, and your bride, there is hope that some of those prayers you have listened to will be happily answered by you. It will depend on your heart and whether you allow your Bride to be open and accessible in speaking and praying.

# So What about Her Heart?

*Some men may have* read this far and feel that you don't know what is on your brides's heart because I have focused on the life experience and possible sins committed against your heart. Your bride's God-created, original heart is extremely similar to yours, judging and functioning by asking the same vital questions. (Do you know what they are yet?) Your bride's heart was tossed into the same world, with a strong possibility of Adam's original sin affecting and warping her heart as it has yours, often producing the same responses you produce. Of course, before meeting you, *her heart* may have been warped by the sins of other people against her, possibly creating warped heart differences—sometimes severe. Is it possible her heart is being warped by you?

It is hoped that by now you are awakened to what has happened to your heart in your life, and have the heart, patience, love of Christ to deal with what is on your bride's heart. If you understand the purpose of this book, you now have many tools to deal with what is on your bride's heart. She is relying on you to be the one to know her. You have a lifetime to do it. In case you are still unsure, I will give you a final tip.

Your bride's heart, like yours, consists of two programs: one with all the good put in it that God wanted and said was good, and the other bad, containing all the sins committed against her. The Old Testament explains that the heart undivided, the whole heart, was the one God made and said was good (Genesis 1:31), and the now-divided heart is the recipient of the original sin from the forbidden fruit. In the New Testament, it is the difference between the old self, the fallen self-divided heart, and the new self that is born again back to the original state your heart was born in.

During communication and especially during arguments, these good and bad programs that make your heart fluctuate and switch back and forth almost instantly, often producing the "I don't understand her" exasperation in your mind. Keep in mind that it also produces the "I don't understand him" response in her mind. Jesus revealed that the devil can somehow get a hold on the bad heart program in all people. When you are having arguments notice in a less emotional way how the communication is occurring, notice the type of words and expressions that flow from the heart's bad program. Notice that the good side of the heart contains the good words, sentences, expressions, and actions. Notice how the bad side of the heart contains all the bad words, sentences, expressions, and actions. Notice they are programmed to flow together seamlessly. When the first word flows from the bad side of the heart, it is almost like you already know the last word that the heart is going to use. Notice how these programs appear in the conversation. Notice how the good and bad fluctuate instantly.

The Bible teaches us how to handle such situations. Learn to control yourself, hold your tongue, and respond with grace, a positive attitude, and forgiveness. Do not be offended. Observe people who don't follow God's wisdom on the matter. Could it be that a conversation between two people is really a conversation between four persons? Could a conversation between a groom and a bride actually be a conversation between the couple's good heart programs and bad heart programs? Four programs operating at once could be causing the confusion that leads to arguments. When arguing with your bride, are you aware of which heart program you are talking to? You need to be aware of which heart program you are choosing to respond from. If you choose the bad side of your heart to respond from, the conversation or argument will simply continue on the bad side of the heart. We see the results of that on the news. Notice when you apply the teachings of Christ and choose to respond with the good side of your heart, marital problems decrease rapidly.

Some hearts have been greatly sinned against. Dealing with your heart and your bride's sometimes can be difficult and get very complicated. Don't be so embarrassed to ask for help in this matter. Some heart problems should not be handled alone. You should not feel ashamed for another person's sin against you.

Take the lead, change your ways if necessary, set a new tone in your household, and become the Christlike example, because now you know better!

## Marching Orders for the Groom

God's marching orders to you as a groom are from a long, long time ago, when the earth was still void. Our Lord was very proud and satisfied when He first created you. He feels that you are special, one of His finest creations. He is so confident in you that He gave you a job, a purpose only you can do. The job is to love, protect, and take care of your precious bride.

More than six thousand years ago, God prepared you for this mission of bonding with your bride's lost heart. He revealed how to do it with His life, death, and resurrection. He sacrificed His life to ensure that you would know how to love your bride. It is a job, planned before the creation of the world, that only you were made to handle. No one else will do. Jesus put you in charge of this.

The problem is that your bride's heart is a mess. It is breaking or broken. God knew it would be, even before Adam and Eve ate the fruit. He gave the warning in Genesis 2:15–17 (NIV):

> The LORD God took the man and put him in the Garden of Eden to work it and take care of it. And the LORD God commanded the man, "You are free to eat from any tree in the garden; but you must not eat from the tree of the knowledge of good and evil, for when you eat from it you will certainly die."

It was death of the perfect original heart God made and said was good. The original whole, perfect, good heart became divided, broken, and confused. God knew Adam and Eve would no longer be able to love. And God, all-knowing and prepared, put enmity between Eve, her offspring, and the devil:

> And I will put enmity between you and the woman, and between your offspring and hers; he will crush your head, and you will strike his heel. (Genesis 3:15 NIV)

God did this because the devil *broke her heart.* God knew this would happen from the very beginning of creation. From the beginning, before the devil was created, God begat an enmity and gave Him a name: Messiah. We know Him as Jesus, and the devil had no idea. Jesus is alive, actively opposed to the devil's breaking of hearts; He is the example, the teacher, of how to mend broken hearts. Learn from Him.

You see, your bride once knew how to love, but sadly *her heart*, like yours and the hearts of many others, has been battered, perhaps even by you. I feel confident in saying that people corrupted her heart, possibly for decades, before she even met you. Her warped heart is put in your hands by order of God Himself. Jesus chose you, not me, not anyone else, to handle this one specific task. He believes you can handle it. He has shown you how. Giving her the love, protection, understanding, and care she has not received from anyone else, as Christ would, will be medicine to her heart. Release your desire for her by showing her your love.

If you follow Christ's plan right, I can tell you how she will feel. She might not admit it, but if she loses you after you have applied so much love from a Christlike state of heart, she will not be the same. But that is not a reason to abuse, loose temper, be prideful, return vengeance, or do anything to hurt her more. God sent you on a mission to love her and know her, and it requires hearing. It is about more than sex, though that is important. It is to know her, outside and inside, and to know *her heart*—to know and provide the things she thinks she wants until she awakens, becomes alive, and realizes that what she wants is you.

Groom, your orders are to imitate Christ and become the enmity between your woman's heart; the devil's hate and confusion. Bring heaven to earth with your bride via *her heart*. If you don't know how, read the manual — the Bible.

# Part Two

# Scriptures and Words
# on Marriage to Ponder

# How Sin Shock
# Affects the Heart

*In this part, I* offer scriptures and words for meditation that can reveal a deep knowledge of how the original God-created heart works. I don't consider them commands, but couples avoid these words at their peril. These may not be easy words to apply, but for those who intend to keep their bride's heart for life, I highly recommend that you make them part of your own heart again.

In the title to this section, I use a phrase that might seem novel: "sin shock." If you have been married for a while, you might already understand what I mean. If you are newly married or about to be, take note that I consider sin shock to be the main reason couples get divorced. It goes like this: a man and a woman want to marry. In the beginning, their hearts are in the right place, and they put forward their best features, efforts, and attitudes. All seems excellent while they are dating—then they get married. Once they are together, they are *shocked* by each other's sins. This is what I call "sin shock." I've explained it more fully in a sermon I published previously, which I reprint following.

### *She Loves Me; She Loves Me Not*

As a sinner saved by grace, I wish to give my conclusion of Genesis 1: 31, Genesis 2, and Genesis 3, based on the knowledge God has given me.

The Bible tells you what was, what is, and what is to come.

Have you read what happened in the beginning?

God created Adam and Eve; all was perfect.

Adam looked at Eve and knew in his heart, because that is the way God made it, that *she* (Eve) *loves me*, and with each heartbeat, he knew, *she loves me*. He thought it over and over: *she loves me*.

And Eve in her heart, in the beginning, knew the same thing: *he loves me, he loves me*. Everything was perfect. *He loves me.*

Then they ate the forbidden fruit, and their fragile hearts changed forever. Their hearts forever played a different beat: *she loves me, she loves me not; he loves me, he loves me not*. And that is how the human heart has beaten since the fall—with few exceptions, you understand.

Our hearts beat the same way today—young, old, rich, or poor, it does not matter who you are—as if our hearts have petals like a flower, and we pull out a petal with every sin we experience. A heart petal pull!

*She loves me, she loves me not. He loves me, he loves me not.*

You can see today that our hearts are a mess. You can understand what it was like between husband and wife after the Fall. You know it is not good.

It's tearing up our hearts. You can see the results in our actions today. People sinning against people. Husbands killing wives, wives killing husbands, parents killing children. Abortion is strong.

People rob people, greed grows stronger, and arguments reign supreme. The one race dividing and taking sides as the devil wants!

People are ready to abuse and destroy one another. Win the

argument at all costs and show no mercy. Fight until the death. Take power however you can. Sacrifice the other person—a neighbor, family, husband, or wife. Make separate groups and let the nations fight until nothing is left.

You see the world around you, and you can see where this is going: pull off every flower petal until the last one is pulled.

*Selah.*

All this started because the first sin resulted in the warping of the heart: *she loves me, she loves me not; he loves me, he loves me not.*

I want to repeat this. Do you remember when you first chose your bride?

You picked her, and she said yes. You know how your heart beat: *she loves me, she loves me, she loves … .* And her heart beat the same: *he loves me, he loves me, he loves me.*

That's the way your heart beats when you choose to marry. Hopefully, your heart survives until the wedding day.

The problem is, 50 percent the marriages had no chance; bride and groom divorced. Why?

One of the reasons is sin shock. That is what I call it.

After marriage, many spouses are shocked by each other's sins. It is our failure to apply the Ten Commandments, but it is also much more. I am talking about all sins that attacked them after their birth until the day they were married—warping their hearts! Sins of their enemies, friends, neighbors, brothers, sisters, fathers, and mothers, chipping away, changing their hearts. Yes, sins mentioned in the Bible but also cultural and family actions and beliefs that may be shocking to another person.

Each husband and wife seem to come into marriage not prepared. They were not taught about marriage by their parents, in their schooling, or in their church. Each is battered by the sins of life. Important: they are revealed when the spouse says in their heart, *He did what? She did what? The family member did what?*

Each husband and wife seem to come into a marriage

convinced that theirs is the way things should be because friends, their country of origin, their culture, and especially their family say so. Right or wrong, life or marriage is done this way.

But are you sure?

Are the ways you are bringing into the marriage what God approved?

Marital tip: try to be aware of the sins committed against you that you bring into the marriage.

Call it sin shock. It resulted from Adam and Eve eating the forbidden fruit.

It is fully documented in the Bible and results in a divorce rate today of about 50 percent even of married Christians. Sin shock results in a warped beating heart. *She loves me, she loves me not; he loves me, he loves me not.*

Will you let sin win?

The Bible reveals that God has been trying to fix our fallen and failing hearts since Adam's fall. You know the problem Adam caused, the change in your past, present, and future.

Do your part as the husband and learn God's techniques! The ones your pastor is trying to teach you. Work smart to try to make heaven come down to earth in your marriage.

Men, if you have studied the Bible but still don't know how to make your marriage work, I understand. The Bible is complicated.

Consider understanding *her heart.*

And consider trying out my previous book, *How to Pick Your Bride and How to Keep Her for Life.* Simplify what the Bible teaches on marriage by using my two concise books. Read, follow, and apply the biblical teaching they provide, and learn how to make your wife's heart beat whenever she experiences you: *he loves me, he loves me, he loves me, he loves me … .*

If you read the Bible as I did when I was young, you quickly scoured the words and spent little time to truly understand what was written. Result: you read a book while getting little out of it, basically missing out on the tremendous amount of information it provided. The Bible provides so much life-helping information in one small book that it can be difficult to absorb. It can be used for everything from food to business,-to medicine, and so much more. So I am asking you to slow down, and consider rereading this book. It you are seeking marriage or help with your marriage, realize how the Bible teaches us how to marry for life. It provides the knowledge for what is needed. That is why pastors have told readers to meditate on scripture, to chew the cud of the scriptures, as the farmers did in ancient Israel.

The second part of this book focuses on scriptures that teach you how to deal with your bride's heart, and how to marry, and though each is short, it should be meditated on. How long? It is up to you. Some may already be part of you. Some you may need to make part of your heart. They are provided by God with the best intentions so you can have what I believe you and your bride always wanted from birth:-Love from someone who wants you, -God and your bride for life. Whether you are aware of your love program or not, love is what you will forever be wanting. The following meditations will help you awaken to that God-created heart you once had—you must be born again—and teach you how to give godly love. -Do your utmost to give godly love, and eventually you will receive godly love. You will receive what you give if not here on earth, in heaven or when Jesus comes. Scour the scriptures for more!

# editation 1

"Do everything in love."
1 Corinthians 16:14 NIV

Is that not why you chose your bride? To assess her heart to love
her better? Let her know your love by doing everything in love.
Assess your heart: what do you have to do to love your bride
better?

# Meditation 2

"We love because he first loved us."
1 John 4:19 NIV

As men believing in God, should we also imitate Him in this matter? Be the first to love? What about as groom? What if there is a marital argument?

Could it be, "I will love her first because Jesus first loved me"?

# *Meditation 3*

"Husbands, love your wives, just as Christ loved the church and gave Himself up for her."
Ephesians 5:25 NIV

Thanks to Jesus, today this scripture is in some ways almost self-explanatory. Many men today willfully choose to die for their bride. But how did Jesus die for us every day of His life? How can you die for your bride every day? -What examples and teachings from Jesus life show us how? What do you have to do or change in yourself to accomplish this daily? -Please consider listing what you have done and what you need to do:

# editation 4

"Love must be sincere."
Romans12:9 NIV

Consider that an insincere heart will mess up her heart, which will mess up your heart.

# ⓜeditation 5

"And over all these virtues put on love, which binds them all together in perfect unity."
Colossians 3:14 NIV

When discerning your bride's heart, remember that love is what she initially wanted. It is essential!

Your love from your original God-created heart is what she has wanted since birth. What types of love does your bride want?

# ℳeditation 6

Jesus said, "But love your enemies, do good to them, and lend to them without expecting to get anything back."
Luke 6:35 NIV

If Jesus expects you to love your enemies this way, how does He expect you to treat your bride, whom you say you love? Can you love your bride's heart in this way?

# *Meditation 7*

"Be completely humble and gentle; be patient, bearing with one another in love. Make every effort to keep the unity of the Spirit through the bond of peace."
Ephesians 4:2–3 NIV

Life might force you to be a roaring lion at the job or outside the home, but at home you should seek to apply this scripture to your fragile bride to try to find rest. Are you making every effort?

Some people may be offended by this biblical truth and boldly lash out with insult and examples of their strength. But they would simply be proving my point by words or actions showing offense, pride, and maybe more coming from the fallen side of their heart. Be not surprised or upset by such responses: they are simply the result of sin committed against them.

I mention this biblical truth to help grooms learn about their bride's broken heart—many men don't know about. Learning *her heart* reveals how you can respond to her heart with love as Jesus would. I hope all those who are married awaken to this truth to avoid damage to the other parts of the fragile human body. As history verifies-, in the Bible a giant was taken down by a small stone.

# *Meditation 8*

"Love is patient, love is kind. It does not envy, it does not boast, it is not proud. It is not rude, it is not self-seeking, it is not easily angered, it keeps no record of wrongs."
1 Corinthians 13:4–5 NIV

This is how to program your heart to set the example for your bride's heart to imitate. Wouldn't you like a bride who treated your heart this way?

# *Meditation* 9

"If anyone says, 'I love God,' yet hates his brother, he is a liar. For anyone who does not love his brother, whom he has seen, cannot love God, whom he has not seen."
1 John 4:20 NIV

You are a liar if you say you love God yet hate your wife. Anyone who does not love his bride, whom you have seen, proposed to, married or are marrying, cannot love God, whom he has not seen.

Am I taking this out of context, or are you?

# *Meditation 10*

"Love does no harm to its neighbor. Therefore love is the fulfillment of the law."
Romans 13:10 NIV

Go ahead and fulfill that law! You married your bride, your closest neighbor. May your heart now know how to be open to your bride's heart. Tread carefully and lightly.

# *Meditation 11*

"But the greatest of these is love."
1 Corinthians 13:13 NIV

It takes love to discern your bride's heart. It takes understanding her heart to know how to love your bride.

# *Meditation 12*

"Love your bride."
John 13:34

Love your bride's heart too. Love is God's medicine for a heart gravely sinned against.

# *Meditation 13*

Jesus said, "My command is this: Love each other as I have loved you."
John 15:12 NIV

Reach up to Christ's heart and love your bride from your heart to her heart.

# *Meditation* 14

"Be merciful, just as your Father is merciful."
Luke 6:36 NIV

When was the last time you offered your bride mercy?

Is mercy something you should consistently offer your bride, the one you love? How often does your Father offer you mercy?

Keep in mind Luke 6:46 (NIV): "Why do you call me, 'Lord, Lord,' and do not do what I say?"

# *Meditation 15*

"And the tongue is a fire, the very world of iniquity; the tongue is set among our members as that which defiles the entire body, and sets on fire the course of our life, and is set on fire by hell."
-James 3:6 IISB-

Consider replacing the word "life" with "marriage". Is marriage part of your life? What does that tell you?

"With it we bless our Lord and Father; and with it we curse men, who have been made in the likeness of God; from the same mouth come both blessing and cursing. My brethren, these things ought not to be this way. Does a fountain send out from the same opening both fresh and bitter water? Can a fig tree, my brethren, produce olives, or a vine produce figs? Neither can salt water produce fresh. Who among you is wise and understanding? Let him show by his good behavior his deeds and gentleness of wisdom."
-James 3:9–13

Consider replacing "we curse men" with "we curse our brides." Are our brides included in this scripture? In my previous book, I wrote that controlling your tongue is important in a marriage, and the subject could be a whole book by itself. It is important to choose your words wisely, especially when you are angry. In general, positive words will return positive words, and negative words will return negative words. Your tongue used loosely will set on fire the course of your marriage, but your precise, positive persistence will be an example for the house.

# *Meditation 16*

"Do nothing out of selfish ambition or vain conceit, but in humility consider others better than yourselves. Each of you should look not only to your own interests, but also to the interests of others." Philippians 2:3–4 NIV

This is a challenging teaching, but I see leaders often fulfilling this scripture. Are you the leader in your household? Will you be or are you head of the house? Would the bride whom you chose to marry fall into the category of "others"? Are you mature enough for such a leadership position? A groom who possesses these traits sets the right example for *her heart.*

# *Meditation 17*

"Do not repay evil with evil or insult with insult, but with blessing, because to this you were called so that you may inherit a blessing." 1 Peter 3:9 NIV

It is a powerful scripture that reveals *her heart*. I believe it would keep many marriages together if consistently applied.

# *M*editation 18

"Put on then, as God's chosen ones, holy and beloved, compassionate hearts, kindness, humility, meekness, and patience, bearing with one another and, if one has a complaint against another, forgiving each other; as the Lord has forgiven you, so you also must forgive. And above all these put on love, which binds everything in perfect harmony. And let the peace of Christ rule in your hearts, to which indeed you were called in one body. And be thankful. Let the word of Christ dwell in you richly."
Colossians 3:12–17 ESV

I can hear your complaints: your bride does not treat you this way. But in this passage, the Holy Spirit is revealing that this was your heart too once. The heart you were born with, created by God.

-God willing, you may have lived long enough to realize that King Jesus treats you this way, becoming compassionate, kind, showing humility, meekness, patience, bearing with you, and loving. Create harmony, peace and be thankful in your marriage. Include forgiveness as part of your heart, remember Jesus is forgiving you when you were not that way for Him. Jesus High Priest holds you responsible, and made you head of household, high priest, and example for your house. It is not easy; it requires a man. But as you learn your role, you will set the example in your house.

-Jesus promises that if you give, you will receive. But what should you give? Give what is in Colossians 3:12-17, and give consistently. Set the example for your bride to experience and eventually learn from. As you lead this way, and set the tone of your household, she will eventually follow. It takes time. The world may have given her, as it did you, the wrong example to follow for years.

-Stop fighting the Holy Spirit and lead with your God-created perfect heart, the undivided heart you were born with. Your bride will be amazed, not knowing what is going on. I can assure you, if you lead with your divided, fallen heart, she will learn and imitate instantly. If you lead with your original God-created heart, God will reward you even if the reward is in heaven. There are many other scriptures in the Bible for you to seek; in there are other love scriptures to give.

# *Meditation 19*

"What will ye that I shall do unto you?"
Matthew 20:32 KJV

In *How to Pick Your Bride and How to Keep Her for Life*, I ask (and ask here again):
Jesus poses the ultimate question that God, your parents, your wife, your children, and other people want to hear: "What do you want?"

# *Meditation 20*

"Know this, my beloved brothers: let every person be quick to hear, slow to speak, slow to anger; for the anger of man does not produce the righteous of God...But be doers of the word, and not hearers only."
James 1:19-20,22ESV

Don't deceive yourself, realize what could happen if these words were applied faithfully to every marriage; your marriage. What peace would applying these words bring to your family? Reconceive in your heart and understand the benefits, if these words were applied to your marriage. Yes they are hard words but don't give up. Keep practicing and become a doer of this word before it is to late for your marriage. Consider writing down which of the previous scriptures you have a problem with and write down how applying these scripture would help your marriage.

# *Meditation 21*

"-For God did not send his Son into the world to condemn the world, but to save the world through Him."-
John 3:17 NIV-

You chose your bride to be an essential part of your personal world. Don't condemn your world but include Jesus Christ and His teachings in your personal world to save it. Learning from Jesus will save your world, and studying about His life on earth will give you the examples needed -to know her heart and teach you how keep her for life.

The example of the Father, Son, and Holy Spirit teaches you how to discern and care for your bride's heart. Consider listing the ways that Jesus, who is single, teaches you about marriage.

# Afterword

I believe our God made all people. When He made each person, I believe He said the same thing of each.

When He made your bride or the woman you want to marry, He looked at her and said, "Perfection." God was delighted and satisfied with His work. But before He let her go, He asked Himself, "Will she see me? Will she look at Me? Will she listen to Me? Will she want Me? Will she Love Me?" Then He sent her to be born.

God put this program in your bride. Since birth, she has quietly asked herself those types of questions daily about everyone she meets. Your bride quietly asks herself that question about *you*, the love of her life, every day, with every experience your bride has with you. She, like God, is constantly measuring you on the scale. Like a baby's heart decipher; she is godlike; she must have those vital questions answered, and the proper answer reinforced often—some brides more than others, and in different ways. These are the same questions God asked of you before He sent you to be born. Some men instinctively know how to answer these questions(love), leading to successful lifelong marriages.

God has been preparing for a Christlike man to be in your bride's life for a long time. If she has married you of free will and without force, I believe she has clearly chosen you to be that Christlike man. She wants *you*. Can you live up to her God programmed want for love? That is what she has been searching for from birth. Many grooms, as many as 50 percent, don't know what it takes to be a groom for life, which is what God wants. I know this because about 50 percent of marriages end in divorce. With this book, you can at least begin your journey to understanding *her heart*, which I hope also will start your journey to understanding *your* heart. Realize that Christ is the king who is coming and that He is listening, loving, patient, and forgiving with what is on your heart. He expects you to be understanding. He wants you to be loving, patient, listening, and forgiving of your *bride's* heart (Matthew 18:23–35). Persistent patience, love, Christlikeness with the knowledge of her heart is what this book is calling for.

Adam and Eve's bodies were different before the Fall. The change God made to their bodies, what we have now, is God's gift to you to encourage you to pursue your bride all your life, helping you to realize who and what is essential in your life. You both demand the "you" program to be fulfilled in your marriage. Marriage is hard and might require some delayed gratification, as Jesus is experiencing now. As leader and head of household, God expects you to take the lead and be the first to choose a Christlike mode in perpetual pursuit of love towards your bride and *her heart*. The Bible reveals critical ways to ensure that you are a husband with Christlike appeal, and I recommend studying it. If you want a quicker read, combining what is taught in this book with my other book, *How to Pick Your Bride and How to Keep Her for Life*, will give you critical Biblical concepts to prepare for and live your marriage. Both books contain teachings and techniques that Jesus revealed to help married men stay married for life. I hope that by reading this book, you now know her heart and will choose to lovingly bless your bride more.

If you are interested in your marriage, scour your Bible—I have tried to be comprehensive, but I am sure I have not covered everything the Bible has to say about your marriage. God bless *her heart* and yours.

*Spiritualfoodpublications.com*
P. O. Box 780197
Maspeth, NY 11378-9997
MichaelBaez@protonmail.com

Highly recommended reading:

HOW TO PICK
YOUR BRIDE
*and*
HOW TO KEEP
HER FOR
*Life*

The Best News for
Adult Christian Males

MICHAEL BAEZ

HOW TO PICK
YOUR BRIDE
*and*
HOW TO KEEP
HER FOR
*Life*

**HARD MOMENTS JOURNAL**

MICHAEL BAEZ

For men who plan to marry or are already married.

Hope you enjoyed your book! We want your opinion on it. Please include your name and email address and the words "OK to Print" in the review you send us.

The Messiah is coming!
Blessed is He who comes in the name of the Lord!

# Notes

# Notes

# Notes

PRINTED IN THE UNITED STATES
by Baker & Taylor Publisher Services

Printed in the United States
by Baker & Taylor Publisher Services